MAGIC TREE HOUSE® FACT TRACKER

Dolphins and Sharks

A NONFICTION COMPANION TO MAGIC TREE HOUSE #9:
Dolphins at Daybreak

BY MARY POPE OSBORNE
AND NATALIE POPE BOYCE

ILLUSTRATED BY SAL MURDOCCA

A STEPPING STONE BOOK™

Random House 🏠 New York

The Magic Tree House Fact Tracker series was formerly known
as the Magic Tree House Research Guide series.

Visit us on the Web!
SteppingStonesBooks.com
MagicTreeHouse.com

Educators and librarians, for a variety of teaching tools, visit us at
RHTeachersLibrarians.com

Library of Congress Cataloging-in-Publication Data
Osborne, Mary Pope.
Dolphins and sharks / by Mary Pope Osborne and Natalie Pope Boyce ;
illustrated by Sal Murdocca.
  p. cm. — (Magic tree house fact tracker)
"A nonfiction companion to Magic Tree House #9: Dolphins at Daybreak."
"A Stepping Stone book."
Includes index.
ISBN 978-0-375-82377-0 (trade) — ISBN 978-0-375-92377-7 (lib. bdg.) —
ISBN 978-0-307-97527-0 (ebook)
1. Dolphins—Juvenile literature. 2. Sharks—Juvenile literature.
I. Boyce, Natalie Pope. II. Murdocca, Sal, ill. III. Osborne, Mary Pope.
Dolphins at daybreak. IV. Title. V. Series.
QL737.C432 O83 2011   599.53—dc22   2011006089

Printed in the United States of America
50 49 48 47 46 45

This book has been officially leveled by using the F&P Text Level Gradient™
Leveling System.

For our mother, Barnette Dickens Pope

Scientific Consultant:

LORAN WLODARSKI, Science Writer, SeaWorld Florida

Education Consultant:

MELINDA MURPHY, Media Specialist, Reed Elementary School, Cypress Fairbanks Independent School District, Houston, Texas

Very special thanks to Will Osborne for his invaluable encouragement and help. We would also like to acknowledge Heidi Johnson of Bisbee, Arizona, one of the best science teachers in America; the staff of the Stockbridge Library in Stockbridge, Massachusetts; Paul Coughlin for his ongoing photographic contribution to the series; and again, our amazing creative team at Random House: Joanne Yates, Angela Roberts, Cathy Goldsmith, Mallory Loehr, and, of course, our editor, Shana Corey, without whose tireless efforts this book could never have been written.

DOLPHINS
AND SHARKS

Contents

Dear Readers,

When we got back from our journey in <u>Dolphins at Daybreak</u>, we really wanted to learn more about dolphins and sharks! So we decided to be fact trackers.

Our fact-tracking was like diving under the sea—and we never got wet! We began in the library. We checked out books and DVDs. Then we looked at many websites. We learned about the different forms of life under the sea. We discovered that coral reefs are like the rain forests of the ocean world. We found amazing information about the way dolphins live together and the way

sharks hunt for food. Finally, we learned that life in the ocean is fragile and needs our protection.

So get your backpacks and your diving suits and let's head for the ocean!

Jack

Annie

1

Oceans

The ocean is a vast and wonderful place. It covers more of the world than land—almost twice as much! In fact, oceans cover 140 million square miles of the earth's surface.

Oceans can be more than six miles deep. Underneath the water, there are great mountains, deep valleys, beautiful coral reefs, and even volcanoes!

Seas are smaller than oceans and are usually no more than 600 feet deep.

13

The ocean is home to dolphins, sharks, and millions of other sea creatures. But life in the ocean is very different from life on land. What is life in the ocean like? What kind of world is it?

Salty Water

Ocean water is very salty. If all the salt in the oceans were spread out over all the land on earth, the salt would be five feet deep. The salt comes from rocks and soil. Rain and rivers wash it from the land into the ocean. Once there, it mixes with ocean water. Most sea creatures need salt water to stay alive.

Layers

Sea creatures live in different depths of water. Scientists call these depths *layers* or *zones*. There are three layers. The top one is called the *sunlit* zone. The middle one is called the *twilight* zone.

Depth means "how deep something is."

And the bottom one is the *midnight* zone.

Most sea creatures we know about live in the first, or sunlit, layer. This layer goes down about 600 feet from the surface. Sunlight shines into this layer, warming the water.

While some sharks eat larger sea animals, they eat plankton as well.

Light from the sun helps tiny sea plants and animals called *plankton* (PLANK-tun) grow in the sunlit layer. Many sea creatures use plankton for food.

Sea turtle

Most dolphins and sharks live here. There are also whales, turtles, squid, jellyfish, and thousands of other *marine* (muh-REEN) animals swimming in the sunlit zone.

Marine comes from Latin and means "of the sea."

Squid

The second layer is the twilight layer. Not much sunlight reaches here. This layer goes down about 3,000 feet. Plants cannot grow. Although some sharks can live at this level, dolphins cannot.

The animals here have adapted to very little light. Some have big eyes to help them see. Others make their own lights with special organs in their bodies called *photophores* (FOE-tuh-forz).

 The spotted ratfish has large eyes to help it see in the twilight layer.

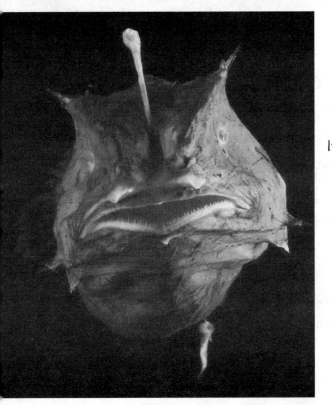

In the midnight layer, the female angler fish catches her prey with the help of a "light" attached to her head.

The third layer is the midnight layer and reaches to the very bottom of the ocean. It goes down over 20,000 feet. It is very dark and cold there. Not a ray of light can shine through. The temperature is almost freezing. Odd and amazing fish live in the midnight layer.

Food Chain

In the ocean, larger and stronger animals eat smaller and weaker ones. Scientists call this process the *food chain*.

Animals at the top of the food chain are called *predators* (PRED-uh-turz). Predators are animals that hunt and catch smaller and weaker animals for food. The animals they eat are their *prey*.

Dolphins and sharks are predators.

Because they are larger and stronger than most sea animals, they are at the top of the food chain.

The smallest and weakest animals near the bottom of the food chain are called *scavengers* (SCAV-in-jurz). They eat leftover bits of plants and animals that are in the water. Scavengers help keep the water clean. In fact, they are like the vacuum cleaners of the sea.

Plankton is at the very bottom of the food chain.

In the food chain, stronger creatures prey on weaker ones.

21

Scavenger →

Most coral reefs are 5,000 to 10,000 years old.

Coral Reefs

Many animals find their food near coral reefs. Coral reefs form near the shore in sunny, warm parts of the ocean. They are made up of the skeletons of small sea creatures called *coral*. After many years, the coral forms tall underwater mountains.

Because reefs are the habitat (HAB-uh-tat) for so many marine animals, scientists call coral reefs the "rain forests of the ocean." A coral reef can look as if it has cliffs, forests, and caves. Some are white, red, orange, yellow, blue-green, and purple. The fish there are often as colorful as the reefs themselves.

Habitat means "the place an animal normally lives."

Turn the page to meet some marine animals of the coral reefs!

Animals of the Coral Reef

The octopus uses its eight tentacles to grab food.

The scorpion fish looks just like a piece of coral. It has poisonous quills on its fins.

The Portuguese man-of-war jellyfish has tentacles up to 165 feet long!

When in danger, puffer fish swell up to twice their normal size.

Sea anemones (uh-NEM-uh-neez) resemble flowers, but they are predators with stinging tentacles.

A sea horse is actually a fish.

2

Dolphins

Marine *zoologists* (zoe-AHL-uh-jists) are scientists who study dolphins and other sea creatures. When zoologists X-ray a dolphin's front flippers, they see bones that look like hands. When they X-ray a dolphin's tail, they see bones that look a little bit like legs.

Because of these findings, most scientists think 50 million years ago, dolphins had hands and legs and lived on land. Over millions of years, dolphins *adapted* (uh-DAP-tid) to life in the water. Their legs turned into strong tails. Their hands turned into flippers. Their bodies became sleek for quick and graceful swimming. They developed ways to breathe in the water and to find food and communicate.

Today there are about 33 different kinds, or *species* (SPEE-sheez), of dolphins. These different species have many things in common.

Cetacea

All dolphins belong to a group of animals called *Cetacea* (sih-TAY-shuh). Scientists think the marine animals in this group lived on land before they began life in the ocean.

Whales are Cetacea, too. In fact, dolphins are just a small type of whale with teeth!

Mammals

All dolphins are mammals (MAM-ulz). Mammals have several important things in common.

People are also mammals.

All mammals are warm-blooded. This means their body temperature stays about the same no matter what the outside temperature is.

All mammals have lungs and breathe air.

Dolphin babies have whiskers when they're born but lose them after birth.

Instead of laying eggs, mammals usually give birth to live babies.

All mammal babies drink their mother's milk.

And all mammals have hair.

29

Mammals

Warm-blooded

Have lungs

Breathe air

Have live babies

Drink milk

Have hair

Swimming

Dolphins are strong swimmers. Most ocean dolphins can swim at a speed of 15 miles per hour. Some have been recorded going as fast as 30 miles an hour!

Dolphins move fastest when they leap out of the water and plunge back in a shallow dive. By making a shallow dive, they spend very little time actually underwater.

This shallow diving is called <u>porpoising</u>.

When they want to dive deeply, some dolphins can go over 1,000 feet deep. When they jump out of the water, they can leap as high as 16 feet in the air.

They get their power from strong tail flukes, which move up and down. Their tails push them through the water quickly—like a motor on a boat.

Dolphins use their front flippers to steer. Some have an upper, or *dorsal* (DOR-sul), fin on their backs that helps keep them upright.

Breathing

Most marine animals get the air they need while swimming in the water. But dolphins have to go to the surface to breathe.

Dolphins breathe through a hole on the top of their heads called a *blowhole*. The blowhole acts like a nose.

Although they can hold their breath for around ten minutes, dolphins usually need to breathe every two minutes.

Dorsal fin

Tail flukes

Just before they reach the surface, they blow all the air from the blowhole. When they reach the surface, they inhale air through the blowhole in less than a second! A flap quickly closes the blowhole, trapping the air, and the dolphins dive back into the water.

Air rushes out of the blowhole at 100 miles per hour!

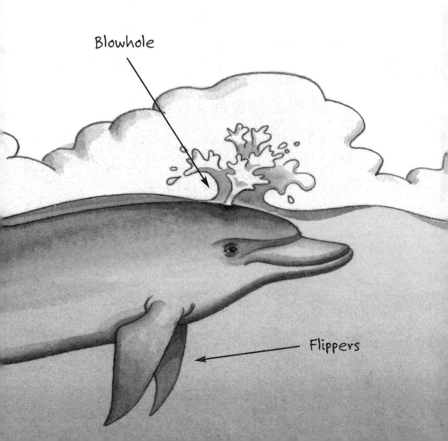

Blowhole

Flippers

Dolphin Skin

Dolphins have smooth skin that feels like rubber. Because their skin is slippery, water flows easily around it. To keep their skin smooth, dolphins shed it constantly.

Dolphins have a special layer of fat under their skin called *blubber* (BLUH-

Dolphins and Porpoises

People sometimes confuse dolphins and porpoises. Here are their differences:

Most dolphins have sharper noses called <u>rostrums</u> (ROS-trumz).

Dolphins have sharp teeth.

bur). Blubber acts like a winter coat and keeps dolphins warm in cold water. Dolphins that live in cold water often have a thicker layer of blubber than those that live in warmer waters.

Blubber is also light and helps keep dolphins from sinking while they swim . . . a little bit like an inner tube!

Porpoises have round noses.

Porpoises have teeth that are flat on top.

Porpoises are usually less than 7 feet long.

Dolphins can be over 30 feet long.

Echolocation

Dolphins find food and communicate with other dolphins by *echolocation* (ECK-koe-loe-kay-shun). This word is made up of two words: *echo* and *location*.

These sounds pass through a part of dolphins' heads called a <u>melon</u>.

Dolphins use echoes to locate fish and other sea creatures they like to eat. When dolphins want to find food, they make clicking or whistling noises. These noises travel through the water and bounce off objects like fish or squid.

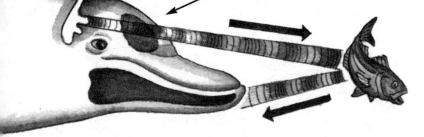

Nasal sacs

Melon

Sound waves are sent through the nasal sacs behind the melon into the water.

Just like an echo, the sound bounces back to the dolphin and vibrates against its inner ear. The dolphin's brain then uses these vibrations to tell the size, direction, speed, and distance of whatever objects are in the water.

Dolphins

Cetacea

Mammals

Strong swimmers

Breathe through blowhole

Smooth skin

Echolocation

Turn the page to learn about different kinds of dolphins!

Killer Whale

Length: up to 32 feet

Weight: 8,000–12,000 pounds

Killer whales are actually dolphins. Although they are not harmful to people, they are one of the most feared animals in the ocean.

Killer whales eat seals, porpoises, birds, whales, and even other dolphins! They can swallow 50 pounds of food in one gulp! Some eat up to 400 pounds of food a day. They hunt in packs of up to 40 and can swim more than 30 miles an hour!

Amazon River Dolphin

Length: six-ten feet

Weight: up to 350 pounds

The Amazon River dolphin is also called the *boto* dolphin. These dolphins are unusual because they can live in fresh water. They are also unusual because some of them are pink! Others are blue-gray.

Every year during the rainy season, the Amazon River floods. Sometimes more than 30 feet of water covers the trees around the river. River dolphins can actually swim through the trees!

Bottlenose Dolphin

Length: up to 12 feet

Weight: up to 1,000 pounds

Bottlenose dolphins look as if they're smiling. They are named *bottlenose* because their noses are shaped like bottles.

Some scientists think bottlenoses are the most intelligent dolphins. Because they learn to do tricks easily, sea parks often train them to leap through hoops or play with balls.

Bottlenoses seem curious about humans and will swim near people in the water. At certain beaches, people can actually swim with trained bottlenose dolphins.

Spinner Dolphin

Length: five-eight feet

Weight: up to 200 pounds

Spinner dolphins are very acrobatic. They get their name because after they jump out of the water, they can spin around as many as 16 times on their tails before diving back into the water again! Besides spinning, they can also do somersaults and other exciting leaps in the air.

Spinners sometimes travel in groups of up to 1,000 dolphins. People often watch spinners off the coast of Hawaii as they perform their amazing spins and leaps.

3

Dolphin Life

Dolphins live together in groups. These groups are called *pods* or *herds*.

A pod has up to 40 dolphins. A herd can have up to several hundred! Beginning at birth, each dolphin depends on other dolphins in the group for survival.

Baby Dolphins

When a dolphin is born, its mother and other dolphins take care of it.

Calves learn to swim about 30 minutes after they're born.

A baby dolphin is called a *calf*. It is born underwater and usually comes out tail first. It can't swim at first, so its mother pushes it to the surface to breathe. Sometimes another dolphin, called an *auntie*, helps the mother do this.

Baby dolphins are around three feet long and weigh 25–50 pounds when they're born.

Calves stay close to their mothers. When calves are hungry, they drink milk from their mother's body. This is called *nursing*. A dolphin baby needs to nurse three to eight times an hour. It nurses for over a year. In just a few weeks, the calf will double in size.

When the baby needs protection, the mother holds it close with her flippers.

Sometimes its older brothers and sisters or grandmother baby-sit.

To teach it her special sound, the mother whistles to the calf constantly for the first two weeks.

When the mother is away hunting, the calf is often watched by an auntie dolphin or other adults in the group.

The calf stays with its mother for as long as six years. During this time, it learns about life in the ocean.

Communication

Dolphins use echolocation to communicate with each other. Each dolphin has its own special way of clicking and whistling.

Baby dolphins first learn to imitate their mother's whistles. Later they develop a special whistle of their own. Dolphins learn to recognize each other by these sounds. When dolphins are together, the ocean is filled with the noise of their clicks and whistles.

Dolphins also communicate by touch. When the mother and baby swim together, they often brush against each other to make sure the other is close by.

If the calf doesn't behave, the mother will push it to the bottom and hold it there a little while. Sometimes the mother even butts the baby's head to show it who's boss!

Dolphin Play

Dolphins spend a lot of time playing together. They even seem to have "best friends." They chase each other. They make circles in the water with bubbles and try to swim through them. They leap out of the

water and fall back in. They slap their tails in the water to get attention.

Since dolphins like the waves boats make, they sometimes swim alongside boats.

Baby dolphins are especially playful. When they play, they throw seaweed at each other. They balance rocks on their flippers. All this play helps them practice skills they'll use later for swimming and hunting.

Hunting

Dolphins hunt together for fish and squid. By acting as a team, they catch a lot more food than they would alone.

Using echolocation, they communicate with each other about where the fish are.

Because fish are easier to catch when they are close together, the dolphins swim in a circle around them. The fish

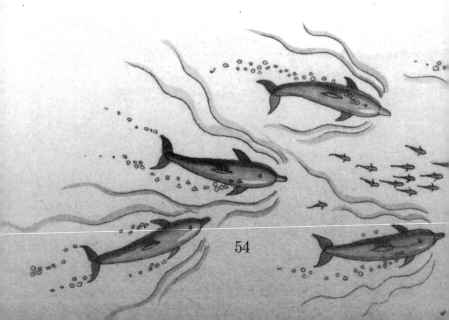

54

move together in a big cluster. Then the dolphins move in for a feast!

Sometimes dolphins spread out in wide groups to catch as many fish as possible. They herd the fish into shallow waters or onto beaches and rocks, where they can't escape. Using their strong flippers, dolphins can pull up to the shore on their stomachs and eat as many fish as they want.

Dolphins to the Rescue

Dolphins protect each other. When a dolphin is in danger, it sends out a distress call. Other dolphins come to the rescue! Sometimes a weak dolphin can't get to the surface. Other dolphins help push it to the surface to breathe.

Dolphins sometimes use their strong tails and sharp teeth as weapons.

When a shark or killer whale threatens the group, stronger dolphins make a protective circle around the weaker ones. Then they drive the predator away by butting it with their hard noses.

56

Dolphins are wonderful creatures. They live and work together. They play together and take care of each other. They do many things people do. But the reason dolphins are amazing is not because they act like people. They're amazing because they act just like themselves!

Turn the page to learn about dolphins and people!

Dolphins and People

For thousands of years, people have been interested in dolphins.

The ancient Greeks believed dolphins were messengers from the gods. They thought killing a dolphin was as bad as killing a human being!

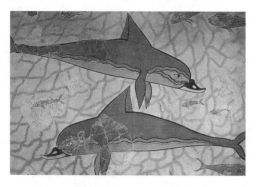

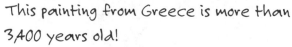
This painting from Greece is more than 3,400 years old!

Many people long ago believed dolphins had special powers. Some thought dolphins could turn themselves into people.

Today everyone knows dolphins can't turn themselves into people. But scientists are learning more every day about what dolphins *can* do.

1. A dolphin can learn simple commands like "get ball." (Sometimes the dolphin won't give it back!)

2. Dolphins also imitate some things people do. Researchers have watched dolphins lift their tails when a person lifted his arms!

4

Sharks

Although dolphins and sharks share the same ocean home, they are very different.

Sharks have been around much longer than dolphins. They came from the first fish, which lived over 500 million years ago! These fish had no jaws or teeth. Over the years, their bodies changed to look like the sharks we know today.

There are more than 350 different species of sharks. Sharks are cold-blooded.

That means their body temperature changes with the outside temperature. Most live in warmer oceans, but some live in rivers, lakes, and even cold arctic seas.

Some sharks lay eggs; others give birth to live young. Some, like the pygmy shark, are small enough to fit in your hand.

Pygmy shark

Whale shark

Others, like basking and whale sharks, are among the largest animals in the ocean and can be more than 50 feet long!

All sharks, however, have important things in common.

Cartilage

Sharks are not mammals. They are a special kind of fish. They belong to a group of marine animals called *Chondrichthyes* (kon-DRICK-thee-eez). Sharks don't have a skeleton made out of bone like most fish. Instead, they all have strong, rubber-like skeletons made out of *cartilage* (KAR-tuh-lidge).

Cartilage feels like bone, but it's not as hard. Because cartilage is more flexible, sharks can turn quickly in the water.

Cartilage is also lighter than bone. This makes it easier for sharks to swim.

Teeth

Sharks have a lot of teeth. Many have five rows of teeth at a time. It's a good thing they have so many teeth because they're always losing them! Adult sharks go through thousands of teeth in their lifetime. When one falls out, a back tooth moves forward to replace it.

Sharks' teeth come in all sizes and shapes. Some are jagged and shaped like triangles; others are narrow and sharp. Scientists can often tell what species a shark is by its teeth.

Shortfin mako shark tooth

Great hammerhead shark tooth

Tiger shark tooth

Shark Skin

Sharks have very rough skin that protects them from injury. It's covered in tiny ridges that are actually tiny teeth! A shark's skin can cause wounds if it brushes against a human or another fish.

In some countries, shark skin is used as sandpaper.

65

Swimming

Sharks are powerful swimmers. They usually swim about one and a half to three miles an hour. But they can swim very fast when they need to.

Most sharks swim by moving their tails, or *caudal fins*, from side to side. Sharks have two fins on their backs that are called *dorsal fins*. These two fins

Some sharks are thought to swim 30 miles per hour! That's as fast as a car!

Caudal fins

Dorsal fins

keep sharks from tipping from side to side. Sharks also have side fins called *pectoral fins* that help lift them up as they swim.

Breathing

Sharks don't have lungs. Instead, they have five to seven pairs of *gills* on either side of their heads. Gills are little openings

Gills are inside gill slits.

Pectoral fins

that filter the oxygen out of the water into the shark's body. Then the oxygen goes into the shark's bloodstream. That allows sharks to breathe underwater—without having to go to the surface. Some sharks swim with their mouths open. This pushes the water back toward the gills.

Scientists used to think that most sharks needed to keep moving through the water to get enough oxygen to breathe. But more than 30 years ago, a discovery changed their minds.

Turn the page to learn what they found!

Cave of the Sleeping Sharks

In 1969, a fisherman swimming off the coast of Mexico came upon an amazing sight . . . an underwater cave of tiger sharks that were not moving! The sharks seemed to be resting, but their eyes were open.

Tiger sharks can be dangerous, but the fisherman was able to get close enough to pet them!

Scientists found the cave had fresh water mixed in with salt water. Fresh water has more oxygen in it than salt water.

They think that the extra oxygen helped the sharks breathe without swimming and perhaps made them calm.

5

Sharks as Predators

Sharks are built to hunt. They move silently through the water, searching for prey. Sharks feast on seals, sea lions, squid, sea turtles, octopuses, other sharks, dolphins, shellfish, seabirds—and lots of fish! When they are ready for a meal, sharks rely on a special group of senses to find food.

Hearing

Sharks have a very keen sense of hearing

and can pick up sounds people cannot hear. They can hear prey moving over a half-mile away!

Much of their food comes from fish that are weak and not swimming well. When sharks hear these fish splashing or swimming unevenly, they swim toward the sound.

Lateral Line

Another sense sharks have is called a *lateral* (LAT-ur-ul) *line*. This is a line of nerves that runs along each side of the shark's body up to its head.

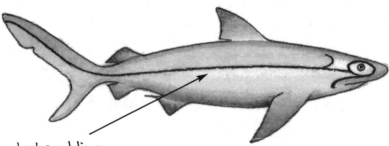

Lateral line

These nerves help sharks feel vibrations, or movements. Sharks can feel vibrations from their prey three to ten feet away.

Sometimes the water is hard to see through. The lateral line helps sharks find their food in murky waters.

It's feeding time for this tiger shark!

Sharks use their noses for smelling, not for breathing.

Smell

Sharks have an excellent sense of smell. In fact, this may be their strongest sense.

Once they catch a whiff of something interesting, they'll follow the scent until they find its source.

Since sharks often prey on weak and wounded fish, they are attracted to the scent of blood. Sharks can sometimes smell a drop of blood from over 1,000 feet away.

By eating weak or dying fish, sharks help keep the ocean clean.

Vision

Sharks have great eyesight! They can see an object more than 50 feet away in clear water. Their eyes are on either side of their heads. This gives the shark a wide view.

Sharks can see as well at night as in the day. Sharks that live in deep waters usually have larger eyes than sharks that live near the surface. Larger eyes help them see objects in the dark.

When some sharks zero in for an attack, they close their eyes or roll them back to protect themselves from being hit in the eye by bones or sharp objects.

Since they can't see, they must use a special sense around the nose to actually hit their target. This sense picks up tiny electrical currents that come from the movements of their prey. Even with their eyes closed, sharks can "see."

When sharks are ready to attack, their jaws unhinge and move forward. The teeth lock into place to give them a better grip on their food. Then they begin to feed.

Sharks

Predators

Good hearing

Lateral line

Great smellers

Sharp eyesight

Turn the page to see what sharks eat!

Sharks Eat the Strangest Things!

Most sharks are actually picky eaters! When they eat something other than marine animals, it's because they've made a mistake. Scientists think the mistake occurs when sharks close their eyes before an attack.

Plastic bag

Shoe

Aluminum can

Anchor

Clothes

Soft-drink bottle

Coal

License plate

W54{3DK

Some amazing things have been found in their stomachs!

6

Shark Attack!

Books and movies often tell stories about sharks attacking people. Sometimes people are even afraid to swim in the ocean. How afraid should they be? How often do sharks actually attack people?

The truth is: not very often. All over the world, millions of people swim in the ocean every day. And yet sharks attack very few people.

You are more likely to be hit on the head by a coconut or stepped on by an elephant than to be attacked by a shark!

Of the more than 350 species of sharks, only 32 are known to attack people.

When sharks attack people, it is usually because they're confused. In fact, sharks are actually shy creatures. Scientists think they mistake humans for sea lions or other marine animals that make up their diet.

Sometimes sharks attack swimmers or surfers. This is because they are attracted to the splashing they hear or to the movement they see—*not* to the people!

These sharks have come close to shore looking for food. They think people in the water are struggling fish.

Spear fishermen have also been attacked by sharks. Sharks are attracted

to blood from the speared fish. Most fishermen take extra precautions. They carry a
special sealed bag to put fish in so sharks
won't swim their way in search of a meal!

Scuba divers swim so smoothly, they often
swim in the midst of sharks without
any fear at all.

Shark Protection

Swimmers can protect themselves from shark attacks. There are many sharks off the beaches of Australia and South Africa. When shark attacks became a problem, nets were put up to protect swimmers. Since then, there have been no further shark attacks.

Scientists are developing sprays that will keep sharks away.

Some divers have experimented with diving suits made of metal to protect themselves from sharks. These might protect against smaller sharks, but they do not work well against large ones. Larger sharks can bite right through the metal.

Diver in metal suit

Here are some ways you can protect yourself when *you're* swimming—with or without sharks!

Safe Swimming

1. Swim in groups.

2. Avoid swimming at dusk or during the night. Many sharks are most active at night.

3. Stay away from sandbars. Sharks sometimes lurk around sandbars looking for fish.

4. If you see a fin moving back and forth, get out of the water.

5. When you're racing to get out, don't splash!

Turn the page to meet some dangerous sharks!

Great White Shark

Length: up to 21 feet

Weight: up to 7,000 pounds

Meet the most feared shark in the ocean! This is the shark in the movie *Jaws*. The great white is huge. But that's not all that's great about the great white. It can have 3,000 teeth!

Great whites rarely attack humans. But they do eat fish, sea lions, seals, otters, and sea turtles. Sometimes, after a big meal, they don't eat for another two months.

Tiger Shark

Length: 10–20 feet

Weight: over 2,000 pounds

Tiger sharks get their name because they have stripes down their back. However, they are dark gray, not tan, like tigers.

These big sharks are sometimes called "the garbage cans of the ocean" because of all the garbage they eat. It seems they'll eat just about anything.

But when they eat too much garbage, they throw up!

Great Hammerhead Shark

Length: up to 20 feet

Weight: up to 1,000 pounds

Great hammerhead sharks get their name because their heads are shaped just like hammers!

As they swim, they swing their head from side to side looking for prey. They might look odd, but having their eyes so far apart helps them see very well. Their heads also help them turn quickly while swimming—like the rudder of a boat.

Great hammerheads sometimes attack humans, but stingrays are their favorite food.

Bull Shark

Length: up to 11 feet

Weight: up to 500 pounds

Bull sharks' faces look a little bit like those of bulls. Their snouts are wider than they are long, and their bodies look almost chubby.

Bull sharks don't swim as fast as many other sharks. And they can breathe while they rest. They are different from most sharks because they live in both fresh and salt water. They live in the Ganges, Amazon, and Zambezi rivers and Lake Nicaragua. They've even been found 100 miles up the Mississippi River!

Bull sharks are aggressive and attack people more often than many other sharks.

Some scientists call them "the most dangerous shark in the world."

Mako Shark

Length: 5-12 feet

Weight: up to 1,000 pounds

Because of their sleek bodies, scientists call makos "the perfect sharks." Their bodies are deep blue and silver and built for speed and grace. Unlike other sharks, the mako can jump high out of the water. Makos swim at the surface of the water and as deep as 1,200 feet.

Some scientists think they are the fastest sharks around. They can travel up to 60 miles an hour for short distances!

7

Saving Dolphins and Sharks

Dolphins and sharks have been swimming in the ocean for millions of years. But today they face great dangers.

Every year over 3,000 dolphins die when they are trapped in huge fishing nets.

Some dolphins are hurt when they try to get out of the nets. Others are killed to prevent them from eating fish that fishermen want to catch. Thousands of other dolphins are killed for food or sport.

Every year, 30 to 100 *million* sharks are killed by nets or for food or for sport. Many are killed for their fins alone.

Shark fin soup is popular in some Asian countries.

Like dolphins, others die when fishermen shoot them as they try to eat fish near the fishing boats.

Ocean Problems

The ocean habitat of dolphins and sharks is also in danger.

Scientists think that noise from boats may interfere with echolocation.

They worry that pollution, garbage, climate changes, and too much fishing are affecting life in the ocean. When bad things happen in the ocean, all marine animals are in danger.

Mini-subs help scientists research the deep ocean habitat.

Research

Scientists are researching dolphins and sharks in order to help them. They use photographs to track dolphins' movements in the water. They track sharks by inserting special tags in their skin. By counting the number of sharks and dolphins living in the ocean and by learning about their ocean habitat, scientists learn how changes in the ocean affect dolphins and sharks.

These scientists are measuring and tagging a lemon shark.

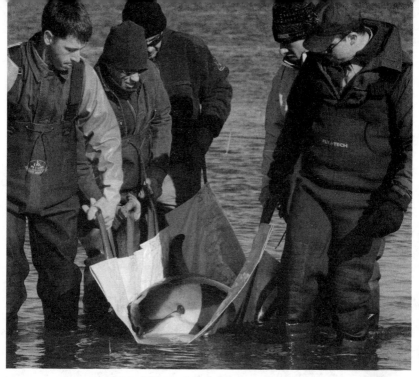

Conservationists in Massachusetts help a stranded dolphin.

Conservation

Scientists and volunteers are also joining together to protect dolphins and sharks. This is called *conservation* (con-sur-VAY-shun). *Conservation* means "to keep things from harm."

Conservation groups are trying to get laws passed to stop too much fishing with huge nets. They are trying to stop the pollution of oceans by chemicals and garbage. Conservationists know that a healthy ocean is necessary for all marine animals.

What Can You Do?

1. You can help by not leaving garbage at the beach.
2. You can ask your parents to buy tuna fish that is labeled "dolphin-safe."
3. You can help recycle and not be wasteful.
4. You and your family can support groups that help marine animals.
5. Your class can write letters asking lawmakers to pass laws that protect the ocean and its creatures.

With your help, sharks and dolphins can

live long lives in their wondrous ocean
home. The more you learn about nature,
the better it is for you—and all the sharks
and dolphins of the world!

Doing More Research

There's a lot more you can learn about dolphins, sharks, and ocean life. The fun of research is seeing how many different sources you can explore.

Books

Most libraries and bookstores have lots of books about dolphins and sharks.

Here are some things to remember when you're using books for research:

1. You don't have to read the whole book. Check the table of contents and the index to find the topics you're interested in.

2. Write down the name of the book.
When you take notes, make sure you write down the name of the book in your notebook so you can find it again.

3. Never copy exactly from a book.
When you learn something new from a book, put it in your own words.

4. Make sure the book is <u>nonfiction</u>.
Some books tell make-believe stories about dolphins and sharks. Make-believe stories are called *fiction*. They're fun to read, but not good for research.

Research books have facts and tell true stories. They are called *nonfiction*. A librarian or teacher can help you make sure the books you use for research are nonfiction.

Here are some good nonfiction books about dolphins and sharks:

- *Dolphins*, Our Wild World series, by Julia Vogel

- *Dolphins*, Smithsonian series, by Seymour Simon

- *Everything Dolphin: What Kids Really Want to Know About Dolphins*, Kids' FAQ series, by Marty Crisp

- *The Everything Kids' Sharks Book* by Kathi Wagner and Obe Wagner

- *Sharks*, Kingfisher Knowledge series, by Miranda Smith

- *Sharks*, Our Wild World series, by Laura Evert

Museums and Aquariums

At many museums and aquariums, you can learn about dolphins and sharks. Sometimes you can even see real ones in action!

When you go to a museum or aquarium:

1. Be sure to take your notebook!
Write down anything that catches your interest. Draw pictures, too!

2. Ask questions.
There are almost always people at museums and aquariums who can help you find what you're looking for.

3. Check the calendar.
Many museums and aquariums have special events and activities just for kids!

Here are some aquariums with dolphins and sharks:

- National Aquarium (Baltimore)

- New England Aquarium (Boston)

- New York Aquarium

- Seattle Aquarium

- Shedd Aquarium (Chicago)

- Steinhart Aquarium (San Francisco)

DVDs

There are some great nonfiction DVDs about dolphins and sharks. As with books, make sure the DVDs you watch for research are nonfiction!

Check your library or video store for these and other nonfiction titles about dolphins and sharks:

- *Private Lives of Dolphins*
  from NOVA

- *Really Wild Animals: Deep Sea Dive*
  from National Geographic

- *Shark*
  from DK Eyewitness DVD

- *Shark Week: The Great Bites Collection*
  from Discovery Channel

- *20 Years with Dolphins*
  from Nature's Kingdom

The Internet

Many websites have facts about dolphins and sharks. Some also have games and activities that can help make learning about dolphins and sharks even more fun.

Ask your teacher or your parents to help you find more websites like these:

- beach-net.com/dolphins/biology.html

- enchantedlearning.com/subjects/sharks

- enchantedlearning.com/subjects/whales

- idw.org

- kids.nationalgeographic.com/kids/animals/creaturefeature/great-white-shark

- kidzone.ws/sharks

- sdnhm.org/kids/sharks/index.html

- teacher.scholastic.com/dolphin/about.htm

- whaletimes.org

Good luck!

Index

114

115

Photographs courtesy of:

*Have you read the adventure that
matches up with this book?*

Don't miss

Magic Tree House® #9
DOLPHINS AT DAYBREAK

It's sink or swim for Jack and Annie when the
magic tree house whisks them off to the middle
of the ocean. Luckily, they find a mini-submarine
on a coral reef. Unluckily, they are about to meet
a giant octopus and one very hungry shark.
Will the dolphins save the day? Or are Jack
and Annie doomed to be dinner?

Enough cool facts
to fill a tree house!

Jack and Annie have been all over the world in their adventures in the magic tree house. And they've learned lots of incredible facts along the way. Now they want to share them with you! Get ready for a collection of the weirdest, grossest, funniest, most all-around amazing facts that Jack and Annie have ever encountered. It's the ultimate fact attack!

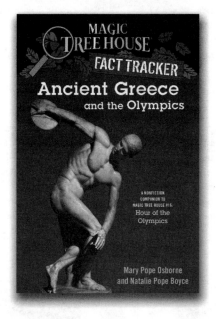

Magic Tree House®

Magic Tree House® Merlin Missions

Magic Tree House®
Super Edition

#1: WORLD AT WAR, 1944

Magic Tree House®
Fact Trackers

More Magic Tree House®

CALLING ALL ADVENTURERS!
Join the
MAGIC TREE HOUSE®
KIDS' ADVENTURE CLUB
Members receive:
• Exclusive packages delivered throughout the year
• Members-only swag
• A sneak peek at upcoming books
• Access to printables, games, giveaways, and more!
With a parent's help, visit MagicTreeHouse.com to learn more and to sign up!
© 2016 Mary Pope Osborne. Magic Tree House is a registered trademark of Mary Pope Osborne; used under license. Illustrations © 2016 by Sal Murdocca.